THE HISTORY OF CRYPTOGRAPHY

THE HISTORY OF
CRYPTOGRAPHY

SUSAN MEYER

ROSEN
PUBLISHING®

New York

Published in 2017 by The Rosen Publishing Group, Inc.
29 East 21st Street, New York, NY 10010

Copyright © 2017 by The Rosen Publishing Group, Inc.

First Edition

Library of Congress Cataloging-in-Publication Data

Names: Meyer, Susan, 1986– author.
Title: The history of cryptography / Susan Meyer.
Description: First edition. | New York : Rosen Publishing, 2017. | Series:
  Cryptography : code making and code breaking | Audience: Ages 7–12. |
  Includes bibliographical references and index.
Identifiers: LCCN 2016017426 | ISBN 9781508173045 (library bound)
Subjects: LCSH: Cryptography—History—Juvenile literature. |
  Ciphers—History—Juvenile literature.
Classification: LCC Z103.3 .M49 2017 | DDC 652/.809—dc23
LC record available at https://lccn.loc.gov/2016017426

Manufactured in China

CONTENTS

INTRODUCTION

When you think of cryptography or encryption, you might think first of cloaked spies, hidden codes, and complex riddles. Codes and ciphers have certainly been used in many of these situations over the centuries. However, you might be surprised to know that you actually use cryptography every day. When you use an ATM at a bank or when you make a purchase online—these tasks are made possible through encryption. It is what keeps sensitive data like banking information safe on the internet. Encryption and cryptography both deal with coded messages or information. Cryptography is the art of writing and solving codes. The word comes from the Greek words "hidden writing." Encryption means encoding a message so that only the correct person can access it. Anyone else who tries to get the message won't be able to.

Over the centuries, encrypting messages has been done in many different ways, from handwritten methods to using simple tools to create codes and finally to the invention of complex machines and computer systems for code making. It's fair to say cryptography has shaped the course of history. From the ancient Egyptians to Julius Caesar and from the Vigenère cipher to the Enigma machine creating codes during World War II, codes and ciphers have long been a way to hide and transport secrets. Codes enable military campaigns to send messages over enemy lines without revealing their plans to the other side. Even during peacetime, coded messages can provide a way to keep sensitive data secret. Codes can provide fun riddles in

People use ATMs to access their cash and bank account information on the go. Encryption is used to keep that sensitive data safe.

literature or in art. They can also help keep your personal information safe, such as by preventing others from accessing your bank account.

The art of code making has evolved over time from when ancient people first started using codes and substituting recognizable symbols for unexpected ones thousands of years ago. Code making had to evolve because as quickly as people can invent new and more complex ways to encrypt messages, other people—known as cryptanalysts—become equally skilled at figuring out how to crack them. Code makers and code breakers are locked in a constant battle. In the process of creating and breaking codes, these innovating cryptographers (or cryptologists) and cryptanalysts have drawn from and inspired new advances in fields from mathematics and linguistics to quantum theory.

Read on to learn not only about the exciting history of code creators from the earliest substitution ciphers in 1900 BCE to modern computer encryption, but also about the people working to crack these codes. How did Alan Turing and the cryptanalysts at Bletchley Park crack the German Enigma machine, forever changing the course of World War II? What is the long-unsolvable Vigenère cipher and how was it solved? What are some of the coolest, most influential codes throughout history and literature? Read on to learn the answers to these questions and many more.

CHAPTER 1

SHIFTY CAESAR AND OTHER CODES FROM THE CLASSICAL AGE

The earliest cryptography or code making dates back almost as long ago as the first writing. The invention of writing enabled people to make messages permanent or semipermanent. It also allowed messages to travel. Suddenly, a person didn't have to be in the same room as someone else to impart information to them. Instead, the message could be written down and passed along by a third party. This opened up the message to new dangers, though. What if someone other than the message's intended recipient were to lay eyes on it? The ancient world was not so different from the modern one in the sense that as long as humans have been around, they have had secrets. Thus, with the invention of writing came the need to hide it and to protect it from prying eyes.

HIDDEN HIEROGLYPHICS

The earliest examples of cryptography date to 1900 BCE in the civilization of ancient Egypt. The Egyptians used a style of writing called hieroglyphics. Symbols called glyphs represented different letters, words, and ideas. Scribes carved these hieroglyphic messages into stone, and some of the messages are still around today. Researchers

The tomb of Khnumhotep II in Beni Hasan, Egypt contains hieroglyphics showcasing one of the earliest examples of a substitution cipher.

discovered that scribes carving hieroglyphics in the tomb of the noble Egyptian Khnumhotep II swapped some of the symbols around. This was perhaps the earliest use of a substitution cipher. A cipher (or cypher) is a secret or disguised way of writing. With a substitution cipher, one substitutes one symbol or character for another. In this case, the scribe substituted normal hieroglyphics with unusual ones, but did so in an organized pattern. This helped hide the message he was writing, but anyone who knew the trick to the cipher could quickly read the message correctly.

Why would the Egyptians have bothered to obscure their writing with easy to solve ciphers? One theory has to do with the fact that only the upper classes in Egypt could read and write. By making their writing harder to understand, they could help protect their messages and rituals from the common people who might have picked up the meaning of a glyph. Another theory is that they did it to provide a fun riddle for people to solve to entice them to read the epithets on tombs or other important messages.

The Egyptians were not the only ancient peoples to try their hand at early ciphering. The civilizations of Mesopotamia, including the Sumerians, Assyrians, and Babylonians, are also known to have used simple forms of cryptography. These civilizations lived in the Fertile Crescent, an area between the Tigris and Euphrates Rivers, in what is present-day Syria, Iraq, and Iran. The Mesopotamians used a style of writing called cuneiform that involves making wedge-shaped lines on stone tablets. A cuneiform tablet found at the site of the former Mesopotamian city of Seleucia (in what is now Iraq) shows the Sumerians' earliest use of hidden codes. The tablet dates to around 1500 BCE, and the writing on it contains instructions for making glaze to decorate pottery. As with the Egyptian hieroglyphics, strange cuneiform symbols are substituted for the expected ones. And as with the Egyptians, the Mesopotamians probably weren't trying to be sneaky. Instead of using encryption as a way to hide the message, they were likely showing off their skills as scribes by adding in unique elements.

It's All Greek to Me

The civilization of ancient Greece also made strides in cryptography beginning around 500 BCE. The Greeks didn't just substitute a few symbols here and there, they developed a special tool for encryption. This device was called a scytale, and the people of the Greek city-state of Sparta were the first to use it. The Spartans were often at war to defend and expand their territory. They needed a way to send and receive secret messages.

The scytale is a wooden cylinder that a piece of thin parchment (paper) can be wrapped around in a spiral. The message that is to be encrypted is written lengthwise around the parchment while it is wrapped around the scytale. When the parchment is unfurled, the message is unreadable. To read the message, the receiver would need a scytale of the same size and width as the one that was used to encode the message originally. A scytale is an early example of what is called a transposition cipher. Unlike a substitution cipher, in which letters or symbols are swapped, a transposition cipher changes the expected order of letters or symbols, essentially scrambling the message around.

There is certain terminology that is necessary for understanding how ciphers and encryption work. The plaintext is the original unencrypted message that is to be hidden. This is the message that would be wrapped around the scytale. The ciphertext is what results after a message has been encrypted and is usually the message that is sent. Looking briefly at a ciphertext, it usually appears like gibberish. Only someone who knows how to decrypt the ciphertext, such as by having the correct corresponding scytale, will be able to untangle the message. Finally, in cryptography, the word "algorithm" means the rules or method used to encrypt a message.

In addition to the scytale, the Greeks also hid messages in other ways. They were known to hide words underneath wax seals. They would also tattoo messages onto the heads of slaves. When the slave's hair grew back, it obscured the message, and the slave could be sent to deliver the message. These intriguing methods are worth noting; however, they are not actually examples of cryptography, but rather a somewhat related field called steganography. Where cryptologists hide a message through codes and ciphers, those using elements of steganography attempt to hide the fact that the message exists at all.

The Caesar Shift

In addition to his strengths as a code creator, Caesar created the Julian calendar, consolidated the power of the Roman republic, and served as its dictator until his assassination in 44 BCE.

The Spartans weren't the only ancient people who were often at war. Between 60 and 50 BCE, Julius Caesar led the Roman army in campaigns across Europe to conquer Gaul (what is now France, Switzerland, and Belgium). Caesar needed a way to communicate with his troops. They were often in enemy lands, so he needed to hide his messages so that prying eyes wouldn't be able to make sense of them. To achieve this, Caesar created a method of substitution cipher that was somewhat more complex than those used by the ancient civilizations of Egypt and Mesopotamia.

Caesar was known to be a clever leader

and problem solver. He came up with his code because he needed to get a message to one of his officers, Cicero. Cicero's troops were under siege and were close to surrendering. Caesar needed to alert Cicero that he and his men would be there soon and that they should hold out; however, if the enemy intercepted this message, they would be prepared for Caesar's arrival. Caesar decided to write the message in Latin (the primary language used by the Roman Empire), but then he substituted Greek letters.

Caesar had more tricks up his sleeve when it came to encrypting his messages. He employed a type of shifting cipher that would become named for him. Basically, he would replace each letter in a text with a letter from a fixed number of places later in the alphabet. For example, if all the letters were shifted three places, then all of the

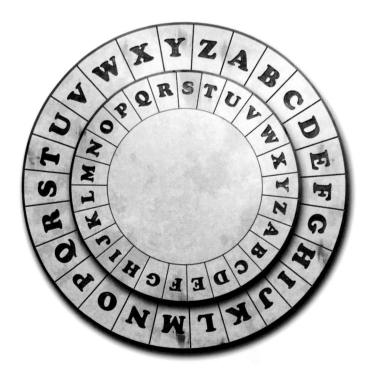

Wheels like this one make it easy to replicate the Caesar shift. One wheel can be moved while the other remains stationary to create the code.

SOLVING THE CAESAR SHIFT CIPHER

Once you know the secret, cracking a message using the Caesar shift is not that difficult! First, you must figure out how many places the letters are shifted. To do this, begin by writing the message. Then write the message as if each letter were shifted one letter. Then write the message as if each letter were shifted two letters. Keep writing different options until familiar words start to appear. That is a strong clue that you have the right algorithm. Once you know the number of letters the message has been shifted, you can easily solve the rest of the message. So, for example, with this message: LIPPS XLIVI

Number of letters shifted:	Message:
0	LIPPS XLIVI
1	KHOOR WKHUH
2	JGNNQ VJGTG
3	IFMMP UIFSF
4	HELLO THERE

By the fourth shift, the message starts to look familiar. Now try it yourself! See if you can decode this message: ILDHYL AOL PKLZ VM THYJO

Answer: BEWARE THE IDES OF MARCH

15

*A*s would become *D*s, all of the *B*s would become *E*s, and so on. While the cipher was fairly easy to figure out by someone who knew the secret, to anyone who didn't, the message would look like garbled nonsense. The Caesar shift allows for some variations, depending on the number of places that the substituted letters are shifted, allowing for anywhere from one to twenty-five places.

The Caesar shift can now be solved easily; however, in Caesar's time it was revolutionary. Because cryptography and substitution ciphers were so new, no one knew what to look out for. However, this would soon change. With the creation of the first codes, the first code breakers would not be far behind.

CHAPTER 2
CODE MAKING AND BREAKING FROM THE MIDDLE AGES TO THE RENAISSANCE

or the first thousand years or so, cryptographers had a pretty good edge. While individual codes and ciphers could be cracked with enough patience, no one had developed a systematic way to solve them. This changed around 750 CE, when Arab people created the field of cryptanalysis, or code breaking. Yaqub ibn Ishaq al-Sabah al-Kindi, known as Al-Kindi and as the Philosopher of the Arabs, discovered a way to break codes through something called frequency analysis. Basically, he realized that in every language, letters appear in certain recognizable patterns and with a reliable frequency. By observing this frequency, he could use the knowledge to crack codes. Al-Kindi published his work in cryptography in a book called A Manuscript on Deciphering Cryptographic Messages.

Using frequency analysis is an excellent tool for any cryptanalyst. Assume that you are trying to decipher a message in English. By knowing the frequency of certain letters that appear in English, you will have a good place to start. For example, the letter *E* is the most frequently used letter in the English language by far. *A* and *T* are next most commonly used letters. Letters like *Q*, *J*, and *Z* are much more seldom used. You can use this information to your advantage!

If you worked out the Caesar shift puzzle in the previous chapter, you know that it could take a while to work through the puzzle by process of elimination. If the message was shifted twenty-three or twenty-four places, you could spend a lot of time working it out through trial and error before you got to the correct word. However, if you knew to look for common letters, you could try and see if the most frequently appearing letter was *E*, and work backwards from there to figure out how many places the rest of the letters had been shifted. This method still takes some trial and error but can dramatically cut down on the length of time needed to solve a code or cipher. Frequency analysis doesn't just work for the Caesar shift but is a good place to start for solving many different types of ciphers.

THE ATBASH CIPHER

While Arab scholars were developing cryptanalysis, in Europe the advances in cryptography were few. The Middle Ages in Europe was sometimes referred to as the Dark Ages because there was less interest in furthering arts and sciences during this time. This included cryptography. The exception was among monks in medieval monasteries. Monks were the most likely to know how to write at this period in history, which in turn made them the most likely to try their hand at secret writing. Medieval monks studied the Atbash cipher. The name Atbash comes from the letters of the Hebrew alphabet. This substitution cipher involves substituting the first letter of the alphabet for the last. The Atbash cipher can be found in the Old Testament of the Bible. In the *Book of Jeremiah*, the word "Sheshach" is used in place of the word "Babel." It is not believed these substitutions were necessarily made to conceal something. They might have been used to add complexity to the text.

While most commonly used for religious purposes, substitution ciphers were occasionally used in other texts during this time. In a scientific text called *The Equatorie of the Plantesis,* which is thought to have been written around 1393, a number of passages include symbols replacing letters of the alphabet in an organized pattern. Again, the writer of the work is thought to have been a monk; however, some scholars also believe the writer Geoffrey Chaucer might have had a hand in the work.

MANY ALPHABETS ARE BETTER THAN ONE

The Dark Ages in Europe was followed by the Renaissance. This period lasted from the thirteenth century to the seventeenth century. During this time, there was a

Geoffrey Chaucer is best known for his work the **Canterbury Tales***; however, he may also have created* **The Equatorie of the Plantesis***.*

rebirth in knowledge and intellectual curiosity, including in the pursuit of creating new and complicated codes and ciphers.

In the mid-1400s, the Vatican—the center of Catholicism and also the home of the Pope—was looking for a way to send encrypted messages. They turned to a man named Leon Battista Alberti. Alberti made contributions to architecture, philosophy, science, and the arts. He was a "Renaissance man," meaning he had many talents and contributed to many different fields. One of these fields was cryptography. Alberti is considered the Father of Western Cryptography because he created one of the first polyalphabetic ciphers.

A polyalphabetic cipher ("poly-" coming from the Greek for word "many") uses multiple alphabets in a grid to encrypt a message. A polyalphabetic cipher is similar to a substitution cipher but because several alphabets are used, it cannot be cracked with frequency analysis alone. This is because each letter in the plaintext could be substituted for several different letters in the ciphertext. The Alberti cipher required a tool that Alberti describes in his 1467 work *De Cifris* (On Ciphers).

The Alberti cipher requires two metal disks that are connected with a common axle. The outer disk is stationary, and the inner disk can be rotated. Around the outside of the stationary disk, the letters

This statue of Leon Battista Alberti stands in the courtyard of the Uffizi Gallery in Florence, Italy. In addition to being a cryptographer, Alberti was a linguist, architect, philosopher, and poet.

of the Latin alphabet are written. The Latin alphabet contains most of the letters of our English alphabet, without *J, U,* and *W.* Alberti also eliminated *H, K,* and *Y.* In addition to these letters, the outer disk also contains the numbers 1 through 4. Meanwhile the inner, mobile disk contains the letters of the Latin alphabet and no numbers, all in random order.

To encrypt a message, both the sender and receiver of the message needed to have the Alberti cipher disks. They would also have to agree in advance on the initial starting place of each disk relative to each other. Then, once the disks were properly lined up, the plaintext message would be read from the outer disk and each corresponding letter on the inner disk would make up the cipher text. So far, it's not so different from a Caesar shift, but Alberti had another trick up his sleeve. After writing an agreed-upon number of letters or words, the sender changes the position of the mobile disk. Again, this is something agreed upon by the sender and the receiver beforehand. So for the first few letters of the message, the plaintext letter *A* might become a *D* in the ciphertext, and later in the same message the *A* might be a *K.* The numbers could also be used to make codes more complex.

CIPHER ON A GRID

Johannes Trimethius was the head of a monastery in Germany. He was the first to come up with the idea of laying out multiple alphabets on a grid to encrypt a message. This grid became known as a Trimethius Tableau. Again, because several alphabets were used, the resulting encrypted message would be harder to crack.

A CODE CRACKED; A PLOT REVEALED

In 1587, Queen Elizabeth was on the English throne and a plot was hatched by some of her enemies to assassinate the queen and put her cousin, the Catholic Mary, Queen of Scots, on the throne in her place. The plan was called the Babington Plot, named for one of its conspirators.

Mary was imprisoned at the time, so it was difficult for those plotting for her release to get messages to her about the plan. They encrypted the messages, and a messenger on the inside smuggled them to the prisoner. Unfortunately for the Babington

This painting depicts the execution of Mary Queen of Scots in 1587 for her part in the plot against Queen Elizabeth. Prior to her execution, Mary had been imprisoned for almost 20 years.

plotters, they were betrayed by a double agent! Their messenger brought the coded letters to a man named Thomas Phelippes, who was fluent in several languages and also familiar with cryptanalysis and frequency analysis. Not only did he crack the code, but he also forged a letter and even encrypted it using the same code the conspirators used. In the letter, he asked Mary to name the conspirators and to swear her cooperation to the plot. Not knowing their code had been broken, Mary revealed all the secrets. She and the conspirators of the Babington Plot were put on trial and executed.

In this case, the cryptanalyst came out on top, and the consequences were deadly.

Although Trimethius was the first to create the idea of the polyalphabetic cipher on a grid, he is not the best known for it. That honor goes to Blaise de Vigenère and his cipher, which went unsolved for several centuries.

CHAPTER 3

SOLVING THE UNSOLVABLE: THE VIGENÈRE CIPHER

By the sixteenth century, encrypting messages using substitution ciphers or transposition ciphers were no longer as useful for keeping messages private. Polyalphabetic ciphers were the future. In the late sixteenth century, a new code would come along that would puzzle cryptanalysts for centuries: the Vigenère cipher. This famous cipher involved the grid used by Trimethius but also the existence of a keyword when using the grid. The cipher was actually first described by another cryptologist, Giovan Battista Bellaso. Bellaso was an Italian cryptographer who first wrote about a version of the cipher in a published work in 1553. This was later misattributed to another cryptographer, Blaise de Vigenère, who also invented a revised version of the cipher in 1586. He is the one the cipher is ultimately most associated with.

Blaise de Vigenère was a French cryptographer and diplomat. He came from a noble family and was educated at prestigious schools in Paris. Vigenère traveled around Europe and spent several years in Rome. While there, he studied the works of other cryptographers, including Bellaso. Vigenère used this knowledge and added to it to create a new cipher in 1586. Vigenère's cipher was what is known as an autokey cipher. This is a cipher that incorporates the plaintext into the key.

How Does It Work?

Like the Alberti cipher and the Trimethius Tableau, the Vigenère cipher is an example of a polyalphabetic substitution cipher. To encrypt a message using this cipher, the cryptographer first needs to create a grid, called a Vigenère square, in which the twenty-six letters of the alphabet create twenty-six columns and also twenty-six rows. If you look at each row, you see that the Vigenère square is really just a series of Caesar ciphers with each row shifting the letters over one more. These are the first three rows of a Vigenère square:

ABCDEFGHIJKLMNOPQRSTUVWXYZ
BCDEFGHIJKLMNOPQRSTUVWXYZA
CDEFGHIJKLMNOPQRSTUVWXYZAB

This pattern would continue through the rest of the twenty-six rows, with the last one ending in *Z*. By having additional alphabets, the cryptographer creates a code that cannot be broken by frequency analysis.

How does it work? First, the cryptographer must choose a key by which to encrypt the message. This key could be a single word or a series of words. As an example, let's say the key that was used was the word *SECRET*. To encode a message using the Vigenère cipher, the cryptographer would first write the keyword as many times as necessary to cover the whole of the message. For example:

```
    A B C D E F G H I J K L M N O P Q R S T U V W X Y Z

A   A B C D E F G H I J K L M N O P Q R S T U V W X Y Z
B   B C D E F G H I J K L M N O P Q R S T U V W X Y Z A
C   C D E F G H I J K L M N O P Q R S T U V W X Y Z A B
D   D E F G H I J K L M N O P Q R S T U V W X Y Z A B C
E   E F G H I J K L M N O P Q R S T U V W X Y Z A B C D
F   F G H I J K L M N O P Q R S T U V W X Y Z A B C D E
G   G H I J K L M N O P Q R S T U V W X Y Z A B C D E F
H   H I J K L M N O P Q R S T U V W X Y Z A B C D E F G
I   I J K L M N O P Q R S T U V W X Y Z A B C D E F G H
J   J K L M N O P Q R S T U V W X Y Z A B C D E F G H I
K   K L M N O P Q R S T U V W X Y Z A B C D E F G H I J
L   L M N O P Q R S T U V W X Y Z A B C D E F G H I J K
M   M N O P Q R S T U V W X Y Z A B C D E F G H I J K L
N   N O P Q R S T U V W X Y Z A B C D E F G H I J K L M
O   O P Q R S T U V W X Y Z A B C D E F G H I J K L M N
P   P Q R S T U V W X Y Z A B C D E F G H I J K L M N O
Q   Q R S T U V W X Y Z A B C D E F G H I J K L M N O P
R   R S T U V W X Y Z A B C D E F G H I J K L M N O P Q
S   S T U V W X Y Z A B C D E F G H I J K L M N O P Q R
T   T U V W X Y Z A B C D E F G H I J K L M N O P Q R S
U   U V W X Y Z A B C D E F G H I J K L M N O P Q R S T
V   V W X Y Z A B C D E F G H I J K L M N O P Q R S T U
W   W X Y Z A B C D E F G H I J K L M N O P Q R S T U V
X   X Y Z A B C D E F G H I J K L M N O P Q R S T U V W
Y   Y Z A B C D E F G H I J K L M N O P Q R S T U V W X
Z   Z A B C D E F G H I J K L M N O P Q R S T U V W X Y
```

cipher	VVVRBACP
key	COVERCOVER...
plaintext	THANKYOU

In this Vigenère table, "COVER" is used as the key word. It is repeated twice to cover the entire message. "VVVRBACP" is the enciphered message, and once deciphered it reveals the plaintext message "THANKYOU."

Key: S E C R E T S E C R E T
Plaintext: WE LEAVE AT D A W N
Ciphertext: OI NVEOW EV UEPF

Each letter of the keyword is used to cycle through the alphabets. For the first letter of the plaintext *W*, you would look at the column topped by the letter *W*, then run your finger down it until you got to the row beginning with *S*, because *S* is the first letter of the key. That letter is *O*, which gives you the first letter of the ciphertext. Using this method makes it harder to find patterns. In the example, the *E* in "We" is first encrypted as an *I* but the *E* in "Leave" is encrypted as an *N*. Because the different letters in the key are what determine the encryption, even the same word repeated throughout would not draw attention to itself.

This cipher was popular because it was easy to learn but difficult to crack. Anyone could create a polyalphabetic grid and encipher a message. And the enciphered message was so difficult to unravel that it became known as the *le chiffre indéchiffrable*, which means "impossible to decipher cipher." A polyalphabetic cipher can't be solved with frequency analysis alone. This particular puzzle resisted solving for centuries.

CRYPTANALYSIS ON THE CASE

It wasn't until the nineteenth century that major advances in cryptanalysis led to the first successful methods of attacking the Vigenère cipher. In 1863, Friedrich Kasiski, a German infantry officer and cryp-

Charles Babbage, seen here, was a British mathematician, philosopher, and inventor. He was one of the first to solve the Vigenère cipher.

tographer, launched an attack against it using a technique that became known as Kasiski's test. He published his work in a book called (when translated from German) *Secret Writing and the Art of Deciphering.* Kasiski's test involves trying to guess the length of the keyword used to encrypt the message. This is done by looking for strings of letters that are repeated. The distance these strings of letters are apart are most likely the length (or multiples of the length) or the keyword. This is because the same word is likely being repeated within the plaintext and happening to fall at the same spot in the keyword. The more repeated strings that are found, the more the code breaker is able to zero in on the length of the keyword. Once the keyword length is established, the cryptanalyst can begin solving the actual ciphertext by lining up a grid the same number of columns as the length of the keyword. Then each column can be treated like a monoalphabetic substitution cipher and frequency analysis can again be used.

It is worth noting that the English mathematician and inventor Charles Babbage actually solved the Vigenère cipher prior to Kasiski. He may have achieved this as early as 1845, but he did not publish his work, as Kasiski did, because his method was considered a military secret.

In the 1920s, William Friedman, a cryptographer in the US Army, discovered another method that could be used to solve the Vigenère cipher, now known as the Friedman test. The Friedman test takes a mathematical and statistical approach to discovering the length of the keyword. He created an equation that uses the index of coincidence to determine the probable

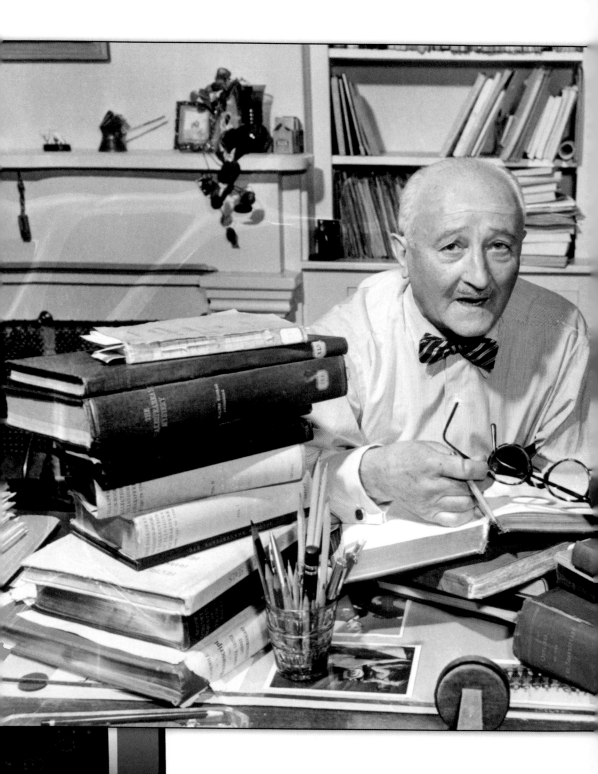

length of the key word. Interestingly, in a way his equation is a mathematically precise approach similar to frequency analysis. Instead of looking at the frequency of letters appearing, the Friedman test considers the probability that two randomly chosen letters are the same.

William Friedman devoted his life to cryptography, serving as a code breaker in the United States Army and later for the National Security Agency. He is known as the "Dean of American Cryptography."

CHAPTER 4

AMERICA TAKES ON CRYPTOGRAPHY

William Friedman wasn't the first or the only American to make strides in cryptography. While thus far, we've focused primarily on the work being done in Europe and the Middle East, the United States also has a long and storied history with code writing and code breaking. The United States was not a country while most of the earliest cryptography techniques were created, but once it became a nation in 1776, the United States had many secrets and intrigues that needed hiding.

FOUNDING FATHER OR CLEVER CRYPTOGRAPHER?

Many are familiar with Thomas Jefferson as one of America's Founding Fathers as well as the third president of the United States. However, he was also a cryptographer, and he created a device for encrypting codes in 1795. He called it a wheel z.

A Jefferson disk is a set of wheels attached to an axle so that they can be spun. Each wheel contains the twenty-six letters of the alphabet. These letters are not in alphabetical order but are scrambled. Each wheel has a unique number and order. Much like the ancient Greek scytale and the Alberti disk, both the sender and the receiver of the message would need a Jefferson disk with the same number and order of wheels on the axle. To

Thomas Jefferson was one of the primary writers of the Declaration of Independence, served as the third President of the United States, and was also one of America's earliest cryptographers.

BITTEN BY THE CIPHER BUG

Edgar Allan Poe was an American writer best known for his poetry and short stories. His stories often featured intriguing mysteries. One of his best-known stories is "The Gold-Bug," which was published in 1843. It tells the story of William Legrand, who is bitten by a gold bug and enlists the help of two friends in unraveling a message that will supposedly lead them to treasure.

The core of the story revolves around the coded message, a substitution cipher. This is a part of the code:

53‡‡†305))6*;4826)4‡.)4‡);806*;
48†8
¶60))85;;]8*;:‡*8†83(88)5*†;46(;8
8*96

The story also includes instructions for solving the cipher, which the characters do in the course of the story. Poe's story was popular and helped make Americans in the nineteenth century become interested in the art of cryptography.

These illustrations are from Edgar Allan Poe's short story "The Gold Bug." The story, published in 1843, was Poe's most popular work during his lifetime.

send a message, the sender adjusts the wheels until the plaintext message appears across the device. Then, the sender looks at the row below the plaintext message (or a row two or three rows below, depending on what has been agreed on with the receiver) to get the encrypted message that is sent. When the receiver gets the encrypted message, he or she knows to line up the wheels on the Jefferson disk to it and then look however many rows above, as agreed on previously, to receive the plaintext message.

The Jefferson disk was considered a strong method of enciphering text at the time of its invention. However, it was relatively easy to break. The codes created are repetitive because the letters and wheels don't change orders, so it is easy for seasoned code breakers to find patterns.

A Country at War

Arguably one of the most influential inventions of the nineteenth century was that of Morse code. Samuel Morse is credited with the creation of a code of lines and dots that made transmission of messages electronically possible. Morse code was not intended to be a secret code, and in fact the codebook for solving it was available to the public. However, the creation of Morse code had a profound influence on cryptography. People developed cryptosystems to encrypt the messages, which would then be sent over the telegraph by a telegraph operator who did not know the code. The message could then be decrypted by the receiver on the other side. Sending encrypted messages would soon become useful because the United States would soon find itself at war... with itself.

The Civil War began in the United States in 1861 and lasted until 1865. The country was split down the middle, with the Union in the North fighting the Confederacy in the South. Both sides could use Morse code and the telegraph to send electronic messages but had to be careful about the messages being intercepted by the enemy. Encryption was used by both the Union and the Confederacy. One example was something called a route cipher, which is a type of transposition cipher in which the plaintext is written on a grid. The algorithm to solving the cipher could be a spiral or a zigzag.

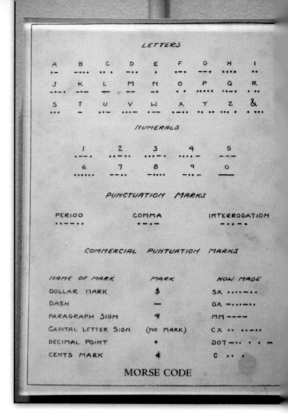

Morse code is a method of transmitting text through short and long tones, lights, or clicks. The basic alphabet is transcribed here in Morse code.

Both the sender and receiver know the correct route. The message can then be sent over the telegraph safely.

CHAPTER 5

THE WORLD AT WAR

A s much of the history of cryptography indicates, wars were a huge incentive for advances in new ciphers and codes and in leaps in cracking them. From Caesar's campaigns in Gaul to modern conflicts, wars invite a strong need for one side to communicate with their men in the war zone without the enemy being able to intercept the message. Never was this more true than in World War I and World War II, two of the defining periods of the early twentieth century. These wars changed the world in a number of ways, and they also changed the world of cryptography.

Z IS FOR ZIMMERMANN

World War I was a conflict involving many of the nations in Europe beginning in 1914 and lasting until 1918. The Allied Powers of Britain, France, and Russia faced off with the Central Powers of Germany and Austria-Hungary. The United States was involved in this war, but only near the end. For much of the war, the United States remained neutral. There were a number of factors that caused the United States to sever its diplomatic ties with Germany and get involved in the global conflict. One of the major factors was the interception of a coded message known as the Zimmermann Telegram.

In January 1917, British cryptanalysts intercepted a message from Arthur Zimmermann, the foreign minister of Germany. The message was a telegram sent to Heinrich von Eckardt, a German foreign minister to

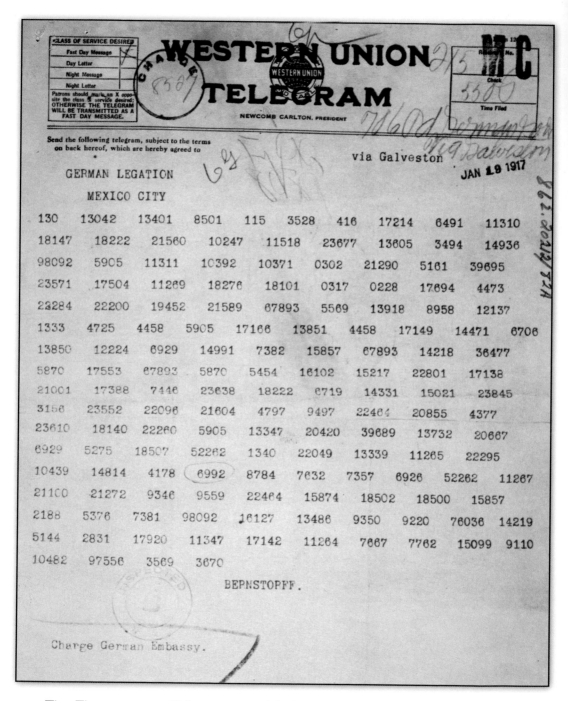

The Zimmermann Telegram would play a crucial role in the war effort. As seen here, the encrypted message was a series of blocks of numbers in seemingly random order.

Mexico. The message was coded using a substitution cipher system the Germans called 0075. The code required one codebook to encipher it and another to decipher the message. The Germans thought this would help increase security. British cryptanalysts working in a part of the British Admiralty known as Room 40 or 40 Old Building were able to break the coded message. The message offered Mexico help in reclaiming land from the southern United States in exchange for Mexico joining the war and offering support to Germany.

This presented an interesting quandary that can happen to cryptanalysts: should you reveal what you know? By revealing the deciphered telegram, Britain would improve the chances that the United States would enter the war against Germany, but they would also be revealing that they had cracked the German's code. By tipping their hand, they ensured that the Germans would use a different code going forward, and they might miss out on more vital information. Ultimately, the British did decide to turn the deciphered telegram over to the president of the United States, Woodrow Wilson, on February 24, 1917. It had the predicted effect: the United States officially declared war against Germany on April 6, 1917. With help from the United States, the Allies would end up winning World War I. Yet again, cryptography changed the course of history.

WORLD WAR II AND THE RISE OF CODE MACHINES

Just two decades after the end of World War I, the world was again engulfed in conflict. Adolf Hitler led

ADFGX

When the Germans realized the 0075 code that was used to encrypt the Zimmermann Telegram had been broken, they realized they needed a new plan. That new plan brought about the creation of a new cipher system known as ADFGX. This code was created by Oberst Fritz Nebel. The cipher got its name because those five letters were the only ones used in the encrypted text. To code a message, the cryptologist first had to create a grid with ADFGX running along the top and down the side. Each letter in the alphabet was laid out on this grid, and each plaintext letter would create a code of two letters depending on its place in the grid (one letter from its column and one from its row). This code was used by the Germans on the Western Front of the war. The code was ultimately broken by cryptanalyst Georges Painvin.

Germany in invading Poland in September 1939, leading to Britain and France declaring war on Germany. The war would grow to involve more than thirty countries and stretch on for six deadly years.

In the years leading up to World War II, there had been a number of advances in cryptography, including the leap from creating codes by hand or using simple manipulative devices like the Jefferson disk to using complex machines. One of these machines was the one-time pad or OTP. With this technique, the plaintext message is encrypted through the use of a secret key. Each letter of the plaintext message is encrypted using a randomly added letter. Gilbert S. Vernam created a one-time pad in 1917 while working at AT&T. Meanwhile, in Europe, Hugo Koch and Arvid Damm both created mechanical rotor-based cipher machines in 1919. By allowing a machine to choose a totally random one-time-use key for enciphering a message, the ciphertext could be made much more difficult—if not impossible—to break.

Perhaps one of the best-known machines from World War II is the German's Enigma machine. This machine was first created by German inventor and engineer Arthur Scherbius. When using the Enigma machine to encrypt a message, the operator scrambles a message using several notched wheels. Each wheel contains

the letters of the alphabet. Meanwhile, the receiver of the message would know the same settings for the rotor wheels and would be able to unscramble the text to get the original plaintext

Enigma machines like this one were sold commercially in the 1920s before being adopted by Nazi Germany to create coded messages during World War II.

message. Over time, the Enigma machine grew more and more complex and its messages were more and more difficult to decrypt. By the 1940s, during World War II, the Enigma machine didn't just have rotors—it also had a plug board (also known as a stecker board) that could be moved around in different configurations. Thanks to the plug board, the number of possible combinations with each rotor were millions. Figuring out how to decrypt messages encrypted by the Enigma machine was a tall order that required years of work from many devoted cryptanalysts.

DEFEATING ENIGMA

Cryptanalysis central during World War II was in a mansion in Bletchley Park in England, 50 miles (80 km) northwest of London. Here clever cryptographers and cryptanalysts cracked codes and helped uncover Germany's secrets. Bletchley Park was home to the Government Code and Cipher School (GC&CS) that was an expansion of Room 40. It was sometimes known by the code name Station X.

At the start of World War II, there were fewer than two hundred people working at Bletchley Park. However, the Enigma machine, the many different ways it could encipher texts, and the increased number of encrypted messages during wartime created a huge workload. By 1945, there were almost nine thousand people working at Bletchley Park. This included many talented mathematicians and linguists from both Britain and the United States. With the huge jump in numbers, huts had to be built at Bletchley Park to accommodate everyone.

The first step to defeating the Enigma code-breaking machine actually happened in the early 1930s, before World War II even began. Three Polish cryptographers realized they could use a mathematical concept called group theory to help break the cipher. This was because at first Enigma used a pattern at the beginning of all messages that was changed on a reliable schedule. Even with a mathematical equation to help, they

The Bombe code-breaking machine, seen here in a photograph from 1943, was used by the cryptanalysts at Bletchley Park to decipher codes encrypted by the German Enigma machine.

still needed to also create a catalog of more than one hundred thousand possible combinations that the Enigma rotors could produce. To help them with this task, they created a machine called a cyclometer. The cyclometer was actually made of rotors from an Enigma machine and helped come up with code possibilities much faster. The Germans changed the way the Enigma machine operated in 1938, and the Polish cryptographers worked to decipher the new method. When Poland was invaded in 1939, they were unable to keep working and sent their work to Bletchley Park.

The cryptanalysts at Bletchley Park had their work cut out for them. To crack the Enigma machine, they needed to predict its rotor settings, which could have millions upon millions of different combinations. The cryptanalyst Alan Turing had a huge contribution to this effort. Turing was a young and talented mathematician, computer scientist, and cryptanalyst. He was born in London in 1912 and had studied at Princeton University in New Jersey. Turing came up with an elec-tromechanical device called a bombe. The approach started by centering on the reliable way that many messages started. For example, many messages actually began with the word "SE-CRET" and messages from German naval operations often began with the ship's position. These words were known as the crib. The bombe could help the Bletchley Park crypt-analysts find the right rotor settings from among eighteen thousand possibilities (still a lot, but quite a bit better than hundreds of millions). The process required a bit of luck, and the cryptanalysts weren't successful every day, but sometimes they landed on the right rotor configurations. The first Enigma message was broken on January 20, 1940, at Bletchley Park. Over the course of the war, they would end up decrypting two and a half million

PURPLE'S REIGN

The Germans weren't the only country to possess a cipher machine during World War II. The Japanese also had one that the United States code-named Purple. The Purple Machine contained two typewriters and had four electric rotors. It was similar to the German's Enigma machine in that the plaintext message could be input through one of the typewriters. Unlike Enigma, which required two people to operate it and thus could increase human error, the Purple Machine could be operated by a single person. The encrypted text was produced automatically by the electric typewriter. The key changed every day, making decryption that much harder. A code sent in multiple parts over multiple days would need several different keys to decrypt.

messages, all while carefully hiding that they had cracked the code. Their contributions to the war effort were immeasurable and without a doubt shortened the length of the war.

CODE TALKERS

American Indians are known to have contributed to the war effort in both World War I and World War II because of their ability to use their own languages as a basis for codes, as well as their talents for creating and remembering codes. According to the National Museum of the American Indian, more than twelve thousand American Indians served in World War I and forty-four thousand served in World War II.

In World War II, the United States Marine Corps recruited Navajo code talkers. The Navajos were known for their ability to maintain secrecy in their communications. While the Navajo code talkers are the best known, members of several other American Indian groups also helped to transmit messages during World War I and World War II. These included the Comanches, Choctaws, Hopis, and Cherokees. The Marines asked them to create code within their languages that could be used for passing messages. After a code was created, more Navajos were recruited and taught the code to memorize. These code talkers provided an invaluable contribution to the war effort. The Navajos helped the United States war effort in Japan, while the Comanches helped against the Germans in Europe.

CHAPTER 6

DECRYPTION IN THE DIGITAL AGE

L uckily, advances in cryptography didn't stop with the end of World War II. Neither did the creation of machines. The last decades of the twentieth century and the first decades of the twenty-first have ushered in a new era: the computer age. With the invention of computers, the field of cryptography and encryption has expanded and changed in many exciting ways.

LUCIFER AND THE DATA ENCRYPTION STANDARD

The Lucifer cipher was created in part by the research of a German cryptographer Horst Feistel. The research was done at the computer company IBM. Lucifer was a machine that was used to encrypt data by applying one encrypting key and algorithm to a block of data. Lucifer was an example of what would come to be known as block ciphers. With Lucifer and other block ciphers, the plaintext message is grouped into sixty-four-bit blocks. (Sixty-four-bit is a measure of computer processing.) Each block is encrypted using the same secret key. To decrypt the message, the reverse is done.

The Lucifer cipher and the research around it led to something called the Data Encryption Standard (DES). This was a type of block cipher that was adopted by the National Bureau of Standards (now the National Institute of Standards and Technology) as the norm for encrypting sensitive information from banking to unclassified government information. The DES made it possible for businesses to send and receive sensitive information securely. The DES was considered the norm from its adoption in 1976 until a stronger algorithm, the Triple DES, became the preferred method in the late 1990s.

PUBLIC-KEY ENCRYPTION

In the mid-1970s, three men working at the Massachusetts Institute of Technology (MIT) came up with a new idea. Their names were Ron Rivest, Adi Shamir, and Leonard Adleman, and their idea would turn into a new cryptosystem called RSA (named for the three men's initials). A cryptosystem is several algorithms working together for one goal, usually security encryption. The RSA cryptosystem ushered in a new era of public-key cryptography.

Public-key cryptography means that a code has two keys, or digital codes. One key is public and the other is kept hidden. RSA is still today the most often used encryption method on the internet. It secures everything from emails to online credit card transactions. How exactly does public-key encryption work? The private key is known to your computer and your computer alone. At the same time, the public key is used by another computer to communicate securely with your computer. Both keys are needed for this com-

Ronald L. Rivest, Adi Shamier, and Leonard M. Adleman, the creators of the RSA algorithm, are seen here at a conference on information security.

munication to happen and for the plaintext data to be received. If Kevin wants to send private data to Jane, he encrypts it using Jane's private key so that only she can access it. The message is secure because only the desired recipient will have the necessary private key. Both keys are based on prime numbers, and there are many different possibilities for keys, making this method of encryption extremely secure.

When visiting your bank online, public-key encryption is used. A secure connection is established with the bank's server before any information is exchanged. The data is encrypted and only your computer's private key can access it. This keeps thieves from accessing your valuable banking information.

THE FUTURE OF CRYPTOGRAPHY

Cryptography shows no sign of stopping in innovation and advancements. One potential advance involves the field of quantum mechanics. Quantum mechanics is a field of physics dealing with the most minuscule parts of the world—down to individual atoms and, even smaller, to subatomic particles. The use of quantum mechanics for encryption is called quantum cryptography. One example of this is quantum-key distribution, which would make an even more secure exchange of keys than currently exists under public-key ciphers. Although RSA ciphers can sometimes be hacked, quantum-key distribution would theoretically be unhackable. The keys would be transferred by photons—tiny

PRETTY GOOD PRIVACY

There are a number of different computer programs for encrypting and decrypting data. These can provide privacy and authentication for communicating data securely. One of the best known is Pretty Good Privacy (PGP).

PGP was created by Phil Zimmermann in 1991. Zimmerman created and made PGP available to raise awareness about the need to protect information online. Once information is put on the internet, it can be easy to lose control of it. By encrypting information before it is sent over email, the sender can ensure that only the intended recipient will see it. Today, PGP is the most widely used email encryption software in the world. It is a form of public-key encryption, and it's generally regarded as extremely safe.

Private individuals as well as organizations can encrypt their emails easily by downloading the free and open-source PGP. Despite the name, the privacy it provides is more than just pretty good.

Making safe purchases online with a credit card is possible because of encryption. Some websites have higher security than others, so it's important to be careful with your information when shopping online.

particles of light—and even if they are intercepted, they can never be perfectly copied. The security of quantum cryptography lies in the very nature of physics and the way our universe operates.

Cryptography has come a long way in the last four thousand years. From simple substitution ciphers to the complex algorithms of the Computer Age, codes and ciphers have evolved to meet the skills of cryptanalysts. The next centuries will no doubt bring new challenges and innovations as today's uncrackable code is tomorrow solved.

GLOSSARY

algorithm The rules or method for enciphering a message.

cipher A way of disguising a message; a code; also called a cypher.

ciphertext A message after it has been encrypted.

crib In cryptography, a word that is expected to be seen in the plaintext.

cryptanalysis The science of solving codes or ciphers.

cryptography The art of writing codes or ciphers.

cuneiform A style of writing used by the civilizations of Mesopotamia that features wedge-shaped characters.

decrypt To break a code to get the plaintext message.

diplomatic Relating to international relations and countries reaching agreements.

encipher To encrypt; to disguise a message.

encryption Hiding a message in such a way that only the intended recipient can read it.

epithet Words of praise, often written on a tomb about the person who has died.

frequency analysis Studying the frequency of letters or groups of letters as a way to break ciphers.

hieroglyphics A style of writing used by the civilization of ancient Egypt in which glyphs represent letters, words, and ideas.

index of coincidence A statistical measure of how a plaintext compares to a ciphertext.

Morse code A method of transmitting text in which letters are represented by long and short bursts of sound or light.

plaintext The unscrambled message, before it has been encrypted or after it has been decrypted.

quantum mechanics The branch of physics dealing with the smallest parts of matter.

scribes People whose job it is to write texts, especially in the time before the printing press.

transposition Changing the word order.

FOR MORE INFORMATION

American Cryptogram Association
56 Sanders Ranch Road
Moraga, CA 94556-2806
Website: http://cryptogram.org
The American Cryptogram Association is a nonprofit collective of people
who enjoy the hobby of cryptanalysis—solving codes and ciphers.
The organization was founded in the 1920s and produces a bimonthly
magazine called The Cryptogram.

Centre for Applied Cryptographic Research (CACR)
200 University Avenue W
Waterloo, ON N2L 3G1
Canada
(519) 888-4567
Website: http://cacr.uwaterloo.ca
Operating as a joint project between the University of Waterloo and the
Canadian government, the CACR promotes the education of cryp-
tographic researchers and the application of cryptographic research,
especially to the field of information security.

Center for Cryptologic History (CCH)
Suite 6886
Fort Meade, MD 20755
(301) 688-2336

According to their website, the CCH provides a "historical and objective
account of cryptologic history." This information is used by the intelligence community, the US Department of Defense, academics seeking
to learn more about cryptography, and the general public.

Communications Security Establishment (CSE)
1929 Ogilvie Road
Gloucester, ON, Canada
(613) 991-7248
Website: https://www.cse-cst.gc.ca
A division of the Canadian government, the CSE's mission is to protect the
government's sensitive information. This includes a group devoted
to signals intelligence (or SIGINT) that intercepts, analyzes, and
decrypts information obtained through electronic signals.

National Cryptologic Museum
8290 Colony Seven Road
Annapolis Junction, MD 20701
(301) 688-5849
Website: https://www.nsa.gov/about/cryptologic_heritage
/museum
The National Cryptologic Museum is a part of the United
States National Security Agency. It includes the history
of cryptology in the United States, particularly as it
relates to national defense.

National Institute of Standards and Technology (NIST)
100 Bureau Drive
Mail Stop 1070

Gaithersburg, MD 20899-1070

(301) 975-6478

Website: http://www.nist.gov

Formerly known as the National Standards Bureau, the NIST is a non-regulatory federal agency under the Department of Commerce. It is charged with advancing measurement science, standards, and technology to improve economic security.

National Security Agency (NSA)

9800 Savage Road STE 6248

Fort George G. Meade, MD 20755-6248

(301) 688-1818

Website: https://www.nsa.gov

The National Security Agency is part of the United States government and leads it in cryptology, including signals intelligence and information assurance. It also maintains records and provides information on US history in cryptography.

WEBSITES

Because of the changing nature of internet links, Rosen Publishing has developed an online list of websites related to the subject of this book. This site is updated regularly. Please use this link to access the list:

http://www.rosenlinks.com/CCMCB/hist

FOR FURTHER READING

Baker, Brynn. *Navajo Code Talkers: Secret American Indian Heroes of World War II.* Mankato, MN: Capstone Press, 2015.

Barber, Nicola. *Who Broke the Wartime Codes?* Portsmouth, NH: Heinemann, 2015.

Berloquin, Pierre. *Breaking Codes: Unravel 100 Cryptograms.* New York, NY: Sterling, 2014.

Blackwood, Gary. *Mysterious Messages: A History of Codes and Ciphers.* New York, NY: Dutton Children's Books, 2009.

Cawthorne, Nigel. *Alan Turing: The Enigma Man.* London, UK: Arcturus Publishing, 2013.

Johnson, Bud. *Break the Code: Cryptography for Beginners.* Mineola, NY: Dover Publications, 2013.

Lonely Planet Kids. *How to Bc an International Spy: Your Training Manual, Should You Choose to Accept It.* Oakland, CA: Lonely Planet Press, 2015.

McFadzean, Lesley. *Creating and Cracking Codes.* New York, NY: PowerKids Press, 2013.

McKay, Sinclair. *The Lost World of Bletchley Park: An Illustrated History of the Wartime Codebreaking Centre.* London, UK: Aurum Press Limited, 2013.

Nez, Chester, and Judith Schiess Avila. *Code Talker: The First and Only Memoir by One of the Original Navajo Code Talkers of WWII.* New York, NY: Berkley Caliber, 2012.

Throp, Claire. *Spies and Code Breakers.* Portsmouth, NH: Raintree, 2015.

Warner, Penny. *The Code Busters Club, Case #1: The Secret of the Skeleton Key.* Minneapolis, MN: Egmont USA, 2012.

BIBLIOGRAPHY

Higgins, Peter M. *Number Story: From Counting to Cryptography.* New York, NY: Copernicus Books, 2008.

Hinsley, F. H. and Alan Stripp. *Codebreakers: The Inside Story of Bletchley Park.* New York, NY: Oxford University Press, 1993.

Gaines, Helen F. *Cryptanalysis: A Study of Ciphers and Their Solution.* Mineola, NY: Dover Publications, 1989.

Janeczko, Paul B. *Top Secret: A Handbook of Codes, Ciphers, and Secret Writing.* Somerville, MA: Candlewick Press, 2006.

Kahn, David. *The Codebreakers: The Comprehensive History of Secret Communication from Ancient Times to the Internet.* New York, NY: Scribner, 1996.

Lunde, Paul. *The Book of Codes: Understanding the World of Hidden Messages: An Illustrated Guide to Signs, Symbols, Ciphers, and Secret Languages.* San Francisco, CA: University of California Press, 2009.

Mollin, Richard A. *An Introduction to Cryptography*, 2nd ed. Boca Raton, FL: CRC Press, 2006.

Pincock, Stephen. *Codebreakers: The History of Codes and Ciphers, from the Ancient Pharaohs to Quantum Cryptography.* New York, NY: Walker Publishing Company, 2006.

Singh, Simon. *The Code Book: The Evolution of Secrecy from Mary Queen of Scots to Quantum Cryptography.* New York, NY: Doubleday, 1999.

Smith, Laurence D. *Cryptography: The Science of Secret Writing.* Mineola, NY: Dover Publications, 1955.

Wrixton, Fred B. *Codes, Ciphers, and Other Cryptic and Clandestine Communication: 400 Ways to Send Secret Messages from Hieroglyphs to the Internet.* New York, NY: Workman Publishing, 1992.

INDEX

ABOUT THE AUTHOR

Susan Meyer is the author of more than fifteen young adult books. She lives with her husband, Sam, and cat, Dinah, in Austin, Texas. She is appreciative of modern encryption standards, as she does most of her banking online. One of her favorite quotes (encrypted, naturally) is: N ebpx cvyr prnfrf gb or n ebpx cvyr gur zbzrag n fvatyr zna pbagrzcyngrf vg, ornevat jvguva uvz gur vzntr bs n pngurqeny. -- Nagbvar qr Fnvag-Rkhcéel

PHOTO CREDITS

Cover, p. 3, interior pages (numbers and letters pattern) © iStockphoto.com/maxkabakov; p. 7 guruXOOX/iStock/Thinkstock; p. 10 De Agostini Picture Library/G. Sioen/Bridgeman Images; p. 13 Jozef Sedmak/Hemera/Thinkstock; p. 14 kprojekt/iStock/Thinkstock; p. 19 GeorgiosArt/iStock/Thinkstock; p. 20 exl01/iStock/Thinkstock; p. 22 Hulton Archive/Getty Images; p. 26 Encyclopaedia Britannica/Universal Images Group/Getty Images; p. 28 Popperfoto/Getty Images; pp. 30 -31 Bettmann/Getty Images; p. 33 GraphicaArtis/Archive Photos/Getty Images; p. 34 Kean Collection/Archive Photos/Getty Images; p. 36 © Ilene MacDonald/Alamy Stock Photo; p. 38 Everett Collection Historical/Alamy Stock Photo; p. 41 Jewel Samad/AFP/Getty Images; p. 43 Bletchley Park Trust/SSPL/Getty Images; p. 49 Kim Kulish/Corbis Historical/Getty Images; p. 52 Ridofranz/iStock/Thinkstock; back cover and interior pages (binary numbers pattern) © iStockphoto.com/Vjom.

Designer: Matt Cauli; Editor: Heather Moore Niver; Photo Researcher: Philip Wolny